Buzzing Bugs

Tom Greve

Rourke
Publishing LLC
Vero Beach, Florida 32964

ISBN-13: 978-0-8249-5144-3
© 2009 Rourke Publishing LLC

All rights reserved. No part of this book may be reproduced or utilized in any form or by any means, electronic or mechanical including photocopying, recording, or by any information storage and retrieval system without permission in writing from the publisher.

www.rourkepublishing.com

PHOTO CREDITS: © eintje Joseph Lee: Cover, Header; © Douglas Allen: page 5, 8, 9; © Viktor Kitaykin: page 6; © Tomasz Pietryszek: page 7; © Janis Litavnieks: page 10; © proxyminder: page 11; © Stefan Klein: page 13; © Jim Dubois: page 15; © Christopher Badzioch: page 17; © Robyn Glover: page 19; © arlindo71: page 20; © Kian Khoon Tan: page 22.

Editor: Luana Mitten

Cover and Interior design by: Renee Brady

Library of Congress Cataloging-in-Publication Data

Greve, Tom
  Buzzing Bugs/Tom Greve
    p. cm.--

Includes Index.
1. Buzzing Bugs--Juvenile Literature. I. Title.

Printed in the United States of America

Table of Contents

Sting or Bite

If you hear a flying **insect** buzzing near you, it might be a good idea to take cover! Most buzzing insects can sting or bite. OUCH!

Bites and stings both hurt. However, there are differences in the ways insects bite and the ways they sting. Stinging insects poke into your skin with a **stinger** that is like a needle. Some insects bite or sting when they feel threatened.

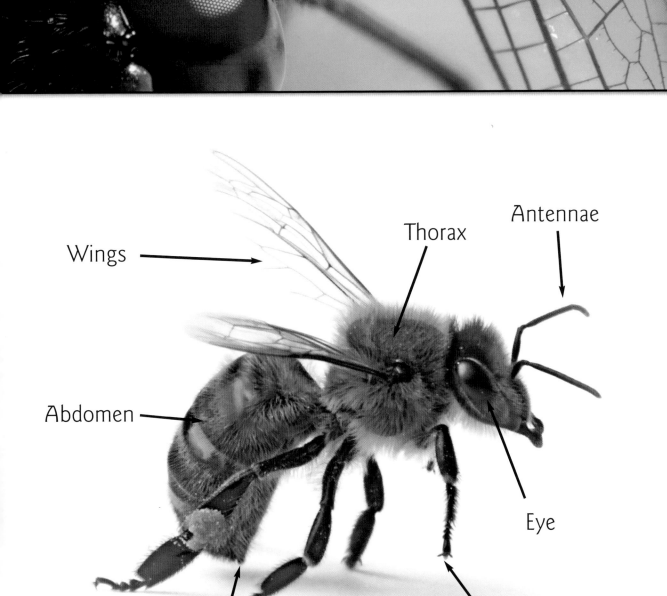

Wings

Thorax

Antennae

Abdomen

Eye

Stinger

Legs

7

Biting insects use their oddly-shaped mouths to bite into their victims. They usually suck the blood of whatever they bite for food. This can hurt because as the insect bites, it injects **toxic** spit, or saliva, into its victim. This often causes the bite to itch afterward.

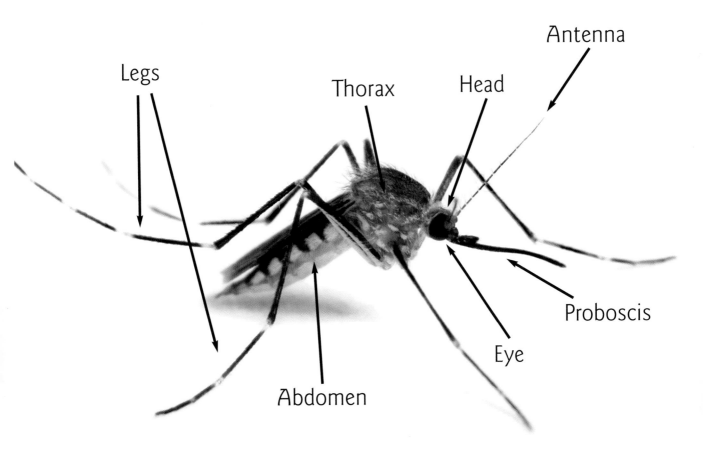

Antenna

Legs

Thorax

Head

Abdomen

Eye

Proboscis

Insects That Buzz and Sting

Buzzing honeybees love to fly around gardens, sucking **pollen** from flowers. They will only sting you if they think you pose a danger. In fact, they die once they use their stinger. So keep your distance!

Buzzing Bugs Facts Bees produce honey and live together in beehives. Beehives have worker bees and a queen bee. The queen's job is to lay eggs. Worker bees build the hive.

Wasps eat insects and even garbage. Unlike bees, wasps can sting over and over. However, they usually will not sting unless you threaten them. So if you see a wasp at a summer picnic, leave it alone.

Buzzing Bugs Facts Wasps are skinnier than bees. They make their nests under overhangs or in some protected areas. Like other kinds of buzzing bees, there are wasp workers and a queen who lays eggs.

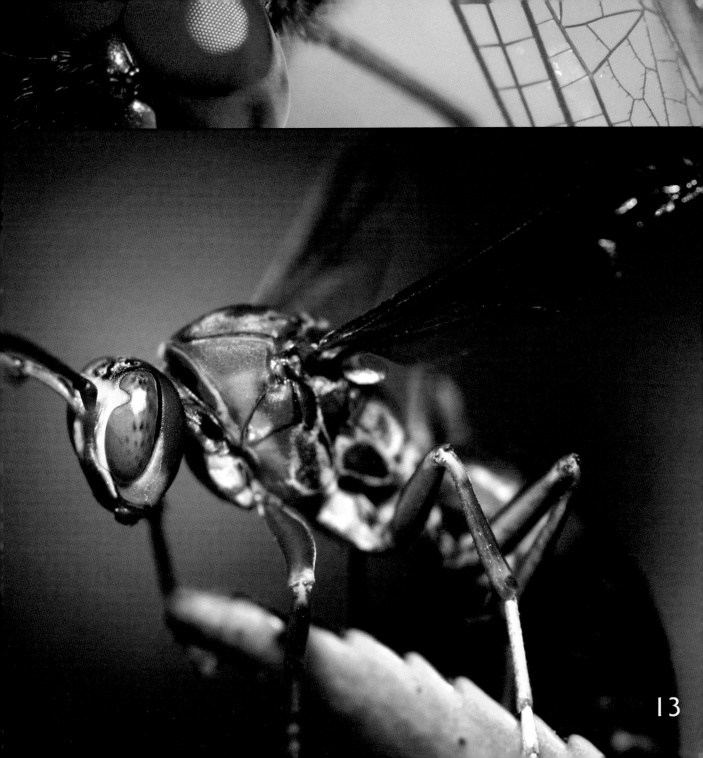

Yellow jackets look like wasps but are more likely to sting. They also can sting over and over. Since they like to eat human food, they can be pests at picnics.

Buzzing Bugs Facts Yellow Jackets live underground, sometimes in holes dug by other animals. Queen yellow jackets **hibernate** in winter, but the males die.

Insects That Buzz and Bite

Perhaps the greatest pest of all buzzing, biting bugs is the mosquito. Female mosquitoes bite and suck the blood of the victim. They leave behind a bump on the skin that itches for days.

Buzzing Bugs Facts Mosquitoes live in dark wet places. They can carry **disease** and make people sick in some parts of the world. They are attracted to dark colors.

Blackflies have hunched backs and wings you can see through. The females bite people, and they sometimes swarm **livestock**. Blackfly **swarms** can kill animals.

Buzzing Bugs Facts Blackflies are smaller than bees but bigger than mosquitoes. They lay their eggs on wet rocks in rivers or streams.

The mouth of a horsefly has two pointy stickers that look like saw blades. The female horseflies bite and suck blood. Males prefer flower nectar.

Buzzing Bugs Facts Horseflies can grow to be an inch long. They love hot weather and mostly live near **marshes** or slow streams.

Are You Allergic?

Most people just get a red, itchy bump from bee stings or bug bites. But a few people have trouble breathing or get very sick. This is called an allergic reaction. You should call 9-1-1 if this happens.

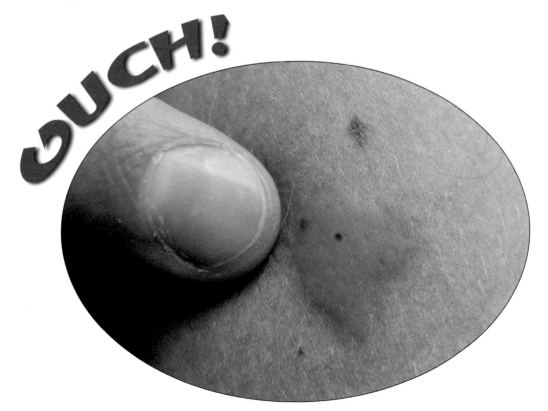

OUCH!

Harmless Buzzing Insects

All buzzing bugs aren't able to sting or bite you. Some insects, like dragonflies, make a buzzing sound as they fly by but they cannot harm you. However, dragonflies are fierce predators known for attacking other insects.

Glossary

disease (duh-ZEEZ): illness

hibernate (HYE-bur-nate): to sleep for a long time, like through the winter

insect (IN-sekt): small creatures with three body sections, wings, and no backbone

livestock (LIVE-stok): farm animals like horses, sheep, or cows

marshes (MARSH-ez): areas of wet, low land

pollen (POL-uhn): tiny yellow grains found in the tips of flowers

stinger (STING-ur): a sharp pointed part of an insect

swarms (SWORMZ): a large group of insects that move together

toxic (TOK-sik): containing poison

Index

Further Reading

Milton, Joyce. *Honeybees (All Aboard Science Reader)*. Grosset & Dunlap. 2003.

Siy, Alexandra, and Kunkel, Dennis. *Mosquito Bite*. Charlesburg Publishing. 2006.

Morgan, Sally. *Bees and Wasps*. QED Publishing. 2007.

Websites

www.biokids.umich.edu

www.tinymosquito.com

insects.tamu.edu

Author info

Tom Greve lives in Chicago. He is married and has two children named Madison and William. He likes being outdoors and riding his bicycle. He once got stung by a bee on his upper lip!